# This Book Belongs To:

_____

_____

_____

# Table of Contents

# Instructions

1. Find a person with whom you can play. If you have more friends who want to join, you can create teams of two (Team A, Team B, Team C, etc.).

2. Agree who should start first. It can be the smartest or the funniest, or you can use rock-paper-scissors if you can't decide.

3. The person or team that starts has to ask the other a Would You Rather question. You have seven chapters from which you can use, each with its difficulty level or specific theme.

4. The other person or team has to choose the best option between the two given scenarios and say why they chose it.

5. Take turns going back and forth while enjoying your funny or honest answers.

6. The game finishes when you ran out of questions, won't be able to make a choice, are tired, or have to do some serious duties. Most probably the latter.

Have fun and loads of laughter!

# Funny & Silly
# Would You Rather Questions

## WOULD YOU RATHER...

never be able to sing when you are in the bathroom

### ⇒ OR ⇐

never be able to dance when you are in the bathroom?

## WOULD YOU RATHER...

get lots of Easter gifts from people you don't know

### ⇒ OR ⇐

get just one Easter gift from your best friend?

# WOULD YOU RATHER...

have chocolate Easter bunnies anytime you need them

## ⇒OR⇐

wish for Easter eggs anytime you need them?

# WOULD YOU RATHER...

have a bed swing in your room

## ⇒OR⇐

a trampoline by the pool?

# WOULD YOU RATHER...

always cough

⇒ OR ⇐

always have a rash?

# WOULD YOU RATHER...

never be able to tell your mum "I'm hungry"

⇒ OR ⇐

never be able to say "I want to play" during Easter?

# WOULD YOU RATHER...

play bunny bowling

≍ OR ≍

play egg bowling?

# WOULD YOU RATHER...

have a bad breath thrice every week of your life
≍ OR ≍

have body odor thrice every week of your life?

# WOULD YOU RATHER...

be tall and chubby

## ⇒OR⇐

short and athletic?

# WOULD YOU RATHER...

have an egg smashed on your face

## ⇒OR⇐

have beach sand poured in your mouth?

## WOULD YOU RATHER...

win an Easter bunny hop sack race

### ⋽ OR ⋜

an Easter egg and spoon race?

## WOULD YOU RATHER...

organize an Easter egg hunt for your friends

### ⋽ OR ⋜

participate in the Easter rolling at the White House?

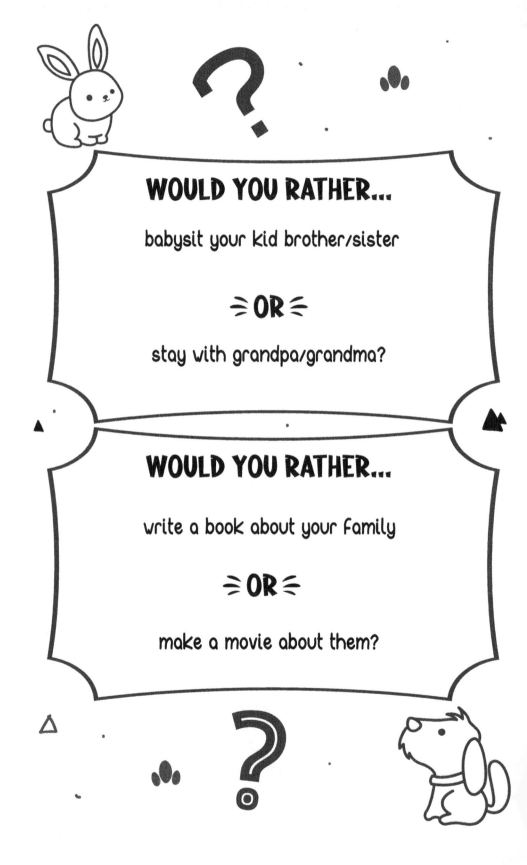

## WOULD YOU RATHER...

babysit your kid brother/sister

≈ OR ≈

stay with grandpa/grandma?

## WOULD YOU RATHER...

write a book about your family

≈ OR ≈

make a movie about them?

## WOULD YOU RATHER...

drink the lemonade that tastes like milk

### ⋛OR⋚

drink milk that tastes like lemonade?

## WOULD YOU RATHER...

play hide and seek

### ⋛OR⋚

get into a pillow fight?

# WOULD YOU RATHER...

play egg-rolling

## ≒ OR ≒

play egg bowling?

# WOULD YOU RATHER...

sleep in a garbage truck for 3 days

## ≒ OR ≒

sleep in a septic tank for 3 days?

## WOULD YOU RATHER...

spend your Easter in a room full of pigs

### ⇒ OR ⇐

spend your Easter in a room full of cockroaches?

## WOULD YOU RATHER...

be stuck in a rollercoaster mid-air

### ⇒ OR ⇐

be stuck on a zip line?

## WOULD YOU RATHER...

dodge the ball

 **OR**

play hide and seek?

## WOULD YOU RATHER...

wake up to see that your Easter chocolate
bunny has become real and living

**OR**

wake up to see your Easter egg had hatched
into Easter chicks?

# WOULD YOU RATHER...

play Easter egg toss

## ⋛ OR ⋚

knock the cans?

# WOULD YOU RATHER...

be one-legged

## ⋛ OR ⋚

one-eyed?

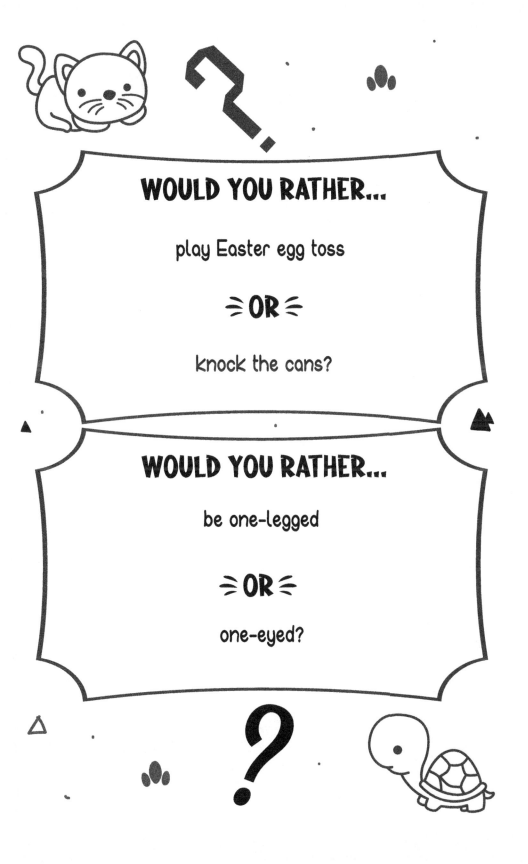

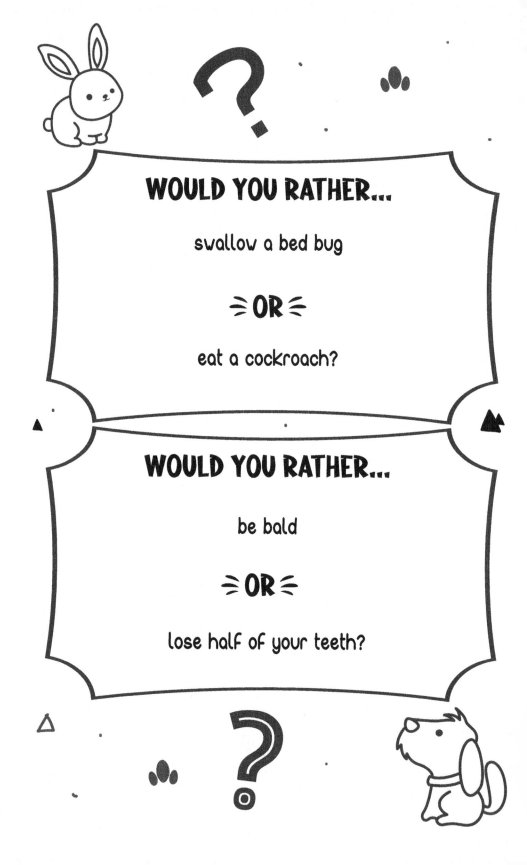

## WOULD YOU RATHER...

swallow a bed bug

≑ OR ≑

eat a cockroach?

## WOULD YOU RATHER...

be bald

≑ OR ≑

lose half of your teeth?

## WOULD YOU RATHER...

Easter grass grew out from your nose

### ⇒ OR ⇐

grew on your teeth?

## WOULD YOU RATHER...

ride a water slide

### ⇒ OR ⇐

a roller coaster

## WOULD YOU RATHER...

never be able to take a photograph during Easter

### ⋛ OR ⋚

never be able to visit your friends during Easter?

## WOULD YOU RATHER...

have a really big toe

### ⋛ OR ⋚

a big protruding navel?

# Easy
# Would You Rather Questions

## WOULD YOU RATHER...

read an interesting story to kids in your neighborhood during Easter

≈OR≈

listen to an interesting story with other kids in your neighborhood during Easter?

## WOULD YOU RATHER...

be 5 years younger but not change in your physical appearance

≈OR≈

5 years older and change in your physical appearance?

# WOULD YOU RATHER...

be stranded in Antarctica

### ⋛ OR ⋚

be stranded in the Sahara Desert?

# WOULD YOU RATHER...

always have to snore

### ⋛ OR ⋚

always have to sneeze?

# WOULD YOU RATHER...

do a bunny hop race with your schoolmates

## ≈OR≈

do the bunny hop race with your neighbors?

# WOULD YOU RATHER...

be able to increase your height

## ≈OR≈

be able to control the length of your hair?

## WOULD YOU RATHER...

be a famous Monarch (like the Queen of England)

≈ **OR** ≈

a famous President (like the President of the United States)?

## WOULD YOU RATHER...

have a tail that can help you fly

≈ **OR** ≈

wings that can grab things?

## WOULD YOU RATHER...

live in Antarctica, where it's cold all day

### ⋛OR⋚

in the desert where it's hot all day?

## WOULD YOU RATHER...

walk through fire without getting burnt

### ⋛OR⋚

walk on water without getting drowned or sinking?

## WOULD YOU RATHER...

make homemade play doughs

≈ **OR** ≈

make tie-dye shirts?

## WOULD YOU RATHER...

be the tallest kid in the world

≈ **OR** ≈

the strongest kid in the world?

## WOULD YOU RATHER...

have desserts

≥ OR ≤

appetizers?

## WOULD YOU RATHER...

be a baby for the rest of your life

≥ OR ≤

never grow older than your current age for
the rest of your life?

## WOULD YOU RATHER...

play look for easy eggs in an Easter hide and seek game

### ≈OR≈

hide the eggs in an Easter hide and seek game?

## WOULD YOU RATHER...

have strawberry ice cream

### ≈OR≈

vanilla ice cream?

## WOULD YOU RATHER...

receive a bicycle as an Easter gift

### ⇒ OR ⇐

a pair of skating shoes?

## WOULD YOU RATHER...

have your own customized robot

### ⇒ OR ⇐

your own customized video game?

## WOULD YOU RATHER...

be a great athlete at 10 different sports

### ⋹OR⋹

be able to speak 10 languages?

## WOULD YOU RATHER...

feed the pets

### ⋹OR⋹

do the laundry?

## WOULD YOU RATHER...

never be able to clean your teeth

≈OR≈

never be able to comb your hair?

## WOULD YOU RATHER...

have an Easter bestie every year

≈OR≈

an Easter squad every year?

## WOULD YOU RATHER...

be able to imitate any voice you heard

### ⇒OR⇐

be able to remember everything you've ever seen?

## WOULD YOU RATHER...

learn to skate on ice

### ⇒OR⇐

learn to skate on land?

## WOULD YOU RATHER...

have a small head that is as small as an apple

≈ OR ≈

have a big head that is as big as a watermelon?

## WOULD YOU RATHER...

speak any language

≈ OR ≈

play any instrument?

## WOULD YOU RATHER...

be a famous comedian or

### ＝OR＝

a superstar actor/actress?

## WOULD YOU RATHER...

have 10 siblings that are exactly your age

### ＝OR＝

10 siblings that are all of different ages?

## WOULD YOU RATHER...

have ninja skills

### ⋛OR⋚

have amazing coding skills in any programming language?

## WOULD YOU RATHER...

travel on the largest ship

### ⋛OR⋚

submarine or the largest plane or hot air balloon?

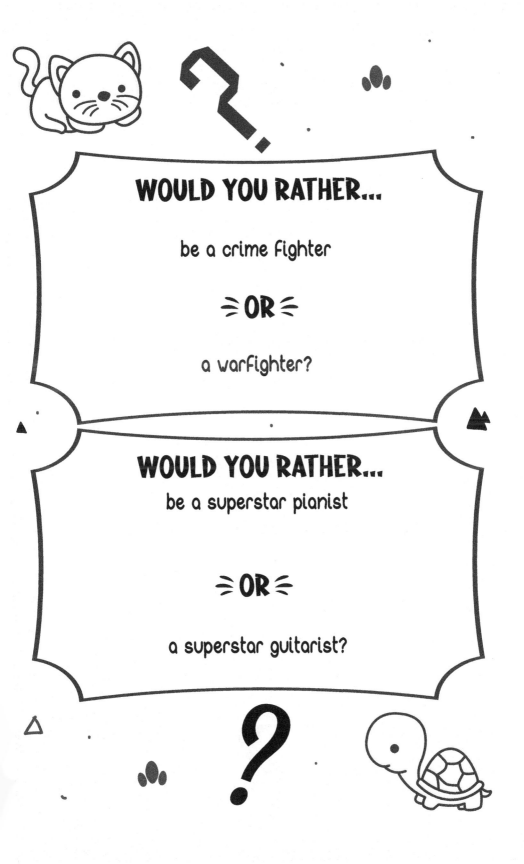

# WOULD YOU RATHER...

be a crime fighter

## ⋝OR⋜

a warfighter?

# WOULD YOU RATHER...

be a superstar pianist

## ⋝OR⋜

a superstar guitarist?

## WOULD YOU RATHER...

travel through time to the best Easter of your life

### ⇒ OR ⇐

travel through time to the best school year of your life?

## WOULD YOU RATHER...

have Easter at the beginning of the year

### ⇒ OR ⇐

the end of the year?

# Hard
# Would You Rather Questions

# WOULD YOU RATHER...

have your diary for Easter posted on social media

≈ **OR** ≈

have your awkward moments posted on YouTube?

# WOULD YOU RATHER...

sleep and not wake up every Easter

≈ **OR** ≈

travel to a faraway land and not see your loved ones every Easter?

## WOULD YOU RATHER...

never be able to use a heater

⇒ OR ⇐

never be able to use an air-conditioner?

## WOULD YOU RATHER...

always have Easter headaches

⇒ OR ⇐

always have Easter backaches?

# WOULD YOU RATHER...

brush your teeth with your soap

## ≈OR≈

use your toothbrush to scrub the toilet?

# WOULD YOU RATHER...

weigh 1 kg but maintain your current size

## ≈OR≈

weigh 500 kg but maintain your current size and appearance?

## WOULD YOU RATHER...

only wear black clothes all through Easter

### ⇒ OR ⇐

only wear white clothes all through Easter?

## WOULD YOU RATHER...

remember everything you have ever heard

### ⇒ OR ⇐

remember everything you have ever seen?

# WOULD YOU RATHER...

lose the ability to stand for more than 2 hours

≈ **OR** ≈

lose the ability to sit for more than 3 hours?

# WOULD YOU RATHER...

help a crying baby

≈ **OR** ≈

help a blind man?

# WOULD YOU RATHER...

sleep on a mountain top

## ≈ OR ≈

sleep by a riverbank?

# WOULD YOU RATHER...

stay awake for a week

## ≈ OR ≈

stay tired for a week (and not be able to sleep)?

## WOULD YOU RATHER...

not have a birthday

=OR=

not have a name?

## WOULD YOU RATHER...

skip Easter for five years

=OR=

spend it alone for five years?

## WOULD YOU RATHER...

have wrinkled skin every Easter

### ⇒ OR ⇐

have brown teeth every Easter?

## WOULD YOU RATHER...

be drenched by an Easter rain

### ⇒ OR ⇐

be sun-scorched?

## WOULD YOU RATHER...

always have to change your friends every Easter

### ⇒OR⇐

always have to change your city every Easter?

## WOULD YOU RATHER...

have the ability to see microscopic things

### ⇒OR⇐

see things very far?

## WOULD YOU RATHER...

not be able to remember your friend's birthdays

## ⇒ OR ⇐

have your friends always forget your birthday?

## WOULD YOU RATHER...

be incredibly lucky with poor intelligence

## ⇒ OR ⇐

incredibly intelligent with no luck?

## WOULD YOU RATHER...

quit video games forever

### ⋛ OR ⋚

quit TV forever?

## WOULD YOU RATHER...

not have water to bathe for a week

### ⋛ OR ⋚

not have water to drink for a week?

## WOULD YOU RATHER...

only be able to walk backward

### ⇒OR⇐

only be able to walk sideways?

## WOULD YOU RATHER...

never be able to say "Thank you!" to anyone

### ⇒OR⇐

never be able to complain to anyone?

## WOULD YOU RATHER...

not be able to talk throughout Easter

### ⋛ OR ⋚

not be able to hear throughout Easter?

## WOULD YOU RATHER...

have a monster as your friend

### ⋛ OR ⋚

an angel as your enemy?

## WOULD YOU RATHER...

have unlimited time on earth but not be rich

### ⋲OR⋵

have unlimited money on earth but not live long?

## WOULD YOU RATHER...

listen to the bad news first

### ⋲OR⋵

listen to the good news first?

## WOULD YOU RATHER...

travel around the world by rail

### ≈OR≈

travel around the world on a ship?

## WOULD YOU RATHER...

be a master of origami

### ≈OR≈

a master of Rubik's cubes?

# Food & Drinks
# Would You Rather Questions

# WOULD YOU RATHER...

not be able to eat roasted turkey every Thanksgiving

## ≋OR≋

not be able to eat roasted lamb during Easter?

# WOULD YOU RATHER...

have free pancakes for life

## ≋OR≋

have free cheesecakes for life?

## WOULD YOU RATHER...

not be able to eat during Easter

### ⇒ OR ⇐

not be able to talk during Easter?

## WOULD YOU RATHER...

eat only wood for a month

### ⇒ OR ⇐

eat only grass for a month?

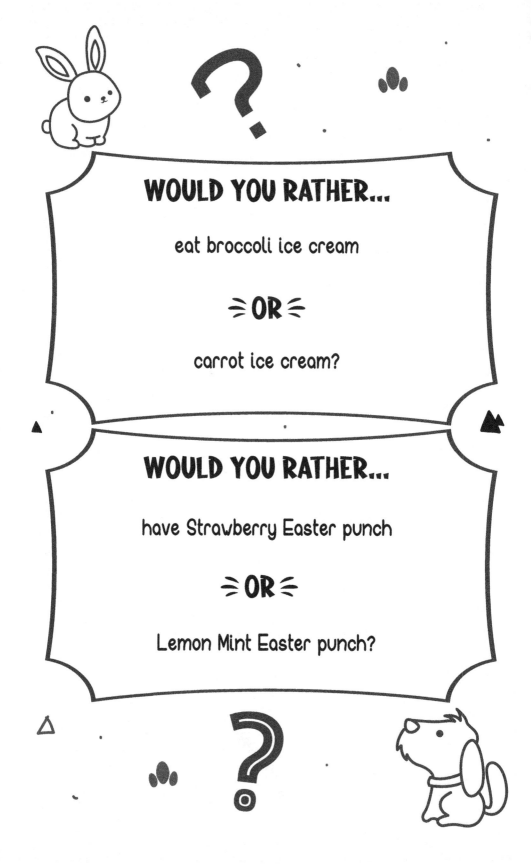

# WOULD YOU RATHER...

eat broccoli ice cream

≓ OR ≒

carrot ice cream?

# WOULD YOU RATHER...

have Strawberry Easter punch

≓ OR ≒

Lemon Mint Easter punch?

# WOULD YOU RATHER...

never have ice cream again

## ≋ OR ≋

never have chocolates again?

# WOULD YOU RATHER...

be trapped on an island with chocolate bunnies
as the only available meal

## ≋ OR ≋

be trapped on an island with Easter eggs as
the only food?

## WOULD YOU RATHER...

eat a whole lemon

≈ **OR** ≈

a raw potato?

## WOULD YOU RATHER...

spend your Easter holiday without food

≈ **OR** ≈

without candies and bunnies?

## WOULD YOU RATHER...

have a spoiled cake smashed in your face

### ≈OR≈

soured yogurt milk poured on your head?

## WOULD YOU RATHER...

eat only mushrooms for a whole day

### ≈OR≈

only pickles for a whole day?

# WOULD YOU RATHER...

eat only mushrooms for a whole day

## ⇒ OR ⇐

only pickles for a whole day?

# WOULD YOU RATHER...

never be sleepy again

## ⇒ OR ⇐

never be hungry again?

## WOULD YOU RATHER...

eat a bowl of spaghetti without sauce

### ⋛OR⋚

a bowl of tomato sauce without spaghetti?

## WOULD YOU RATHER...

eat Easter hamburgers

### ⋛OR⋚

cheeseburgers?

## WOULD YOU RATHER...

have someone chose for you every piece of clothing you would wear during Easter

### ⪦ OR ⪧

chose every food you would eat during Easter?

## WOULD YOU RATHER...

have to eat through your nose

### ⪦ OR ⪧

have to eat through your ear?

## WOULD YOU RATHER...

take Kit Kat wafers to school every day

⇒ OR ⇐

Snickers chocolate?

## WOULD YOU RATHER...

eat hot wings

⇒ OR ⇐

mozzarella sticks at an outdoor event?

## WOULD YOU RATHER...

eat a soap that tastes like a cake

### ⇒OR⇐

eat a cake that tastes like soap?

## WOULD YOU RATHER...

create your own new Easter toy

### ⇒OR⇐

develop your own Easter meal?

# WOULD YOU RATHER...

live on a volcano island

## ≈OR≈

live on a snake island?

# WOULD YOU RATHER...

have a bread and jam breakfast every day
before school

## ≈OR≈

a bread and honey breakfast every day
before school?

## WOULD YOU RATHER...

never be able to eat hot food again

### ≈ OR ≈

never be able to eat cold food again?

## WOULD YOU RATHER...

not be able to eat pizza forever

### ≈ OR ≈

not be able to eat sandwiches forever?

## WOULD YOU RATHER...

never be able to eat cheese again

### ⇒ OR ⇐

never be able to eat biscuits again?

## WOULD YOU RATHER...

be banned from eating Easter jellybeans

### ⇒ OR ⇐

from eating Easter chocolate bunnies?

# Animals & Plants
# Would You Rather Questions

## WOULD YOU RATHER...

have to kiss a dog

### ⇒OR⇐

kiss a cat when you lose an Easter game?

## WOULD YOU RATHER...

be the child of a crocodile

### ⇒OR⇐

the child of a shark?

## WOULD YOU RATHER...

be able to make animals grow faster

### ⇒ OR ⇐

be able to make plants grow faster?

## WOULD YOU RATHER...

be a dog trainer

### ⇒ OR ⇐

lion tamer?

## WOULD YOU RATHER...

have the power to call any animal of your choice on Easter

### ⩵OR⩵

have the power to make any flower of your choice grow?

## WOULD YOU RATHER...

be a friend of an eagle

### ⩵OR⩵

a friend of a bear?

## WOULD YOU RATHER...

have a koala as a pet

≈ **OR** ≈

a giraffe as a pet?

## WOULD YOU RATHER...

have animals greeting you "Happy Easter"

≈ **OR** ≈

have "Happy Easter" messages written to you by different trees?

# WOULD YOU RATHER...

spend your Easter with an animal you hate

## ⋚OR⋚

spend your Easter in a large cornfield?

# WOULD YOU RATHER...

be hopping around like a kangaroo everywhere you go

## ⋚OR⋚

walking slowly like a tortoise everywhere you go?

# WOULD YOU RATHER...

watch animals in a zoo

## ⇒OR⇐

watch animals in the wild?

# WOULD YOU RATHER...

be able to see spirits

## ⇒OR⇐

be able to hear animals talk?

## WOULD YOU RATHER...

spend Easter in a jungle full of nice wild animals

### ≥OR≤

on a tree with talking plants?

## WOULD YOU RATHER...

have the ears of a monkey

### ≥OR≤

have the mouth of a bunny?

## WOULD YOU RATHER...

have all the animals in the world depend on you to save them

### ⇒ OR ⇐

have all the plants in the world depend on you to save them?

## WOULD YOU RATHER...

spend your Easter with animals in the zoo with no light

### ⇒ OR ⇐

spend your Easter with animals in the wild with no food?

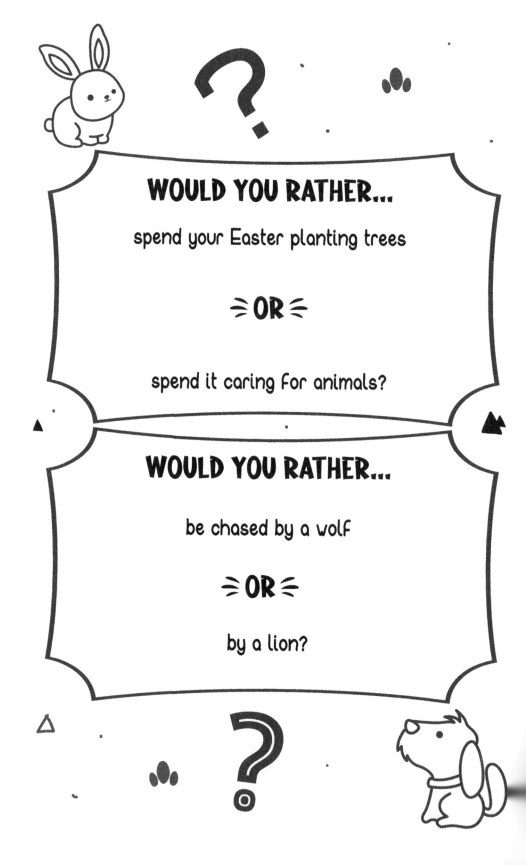

## WOULD YOU RATHER...

spend your Easter planting trees

≈OR≈

spend it caring for animals?

## WOULD YOU RATHER...

be chased by a wolf

≈OR≈

by a lion?

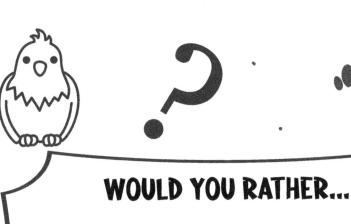

## WOULD YOU RATHER...

be stung by a hornet

### ≈ OR ≈

stung by a scorpion?

## WOULD YOU RATHER...

be chased by a bunny

### ≈ OR ≈

chased by a chicken?

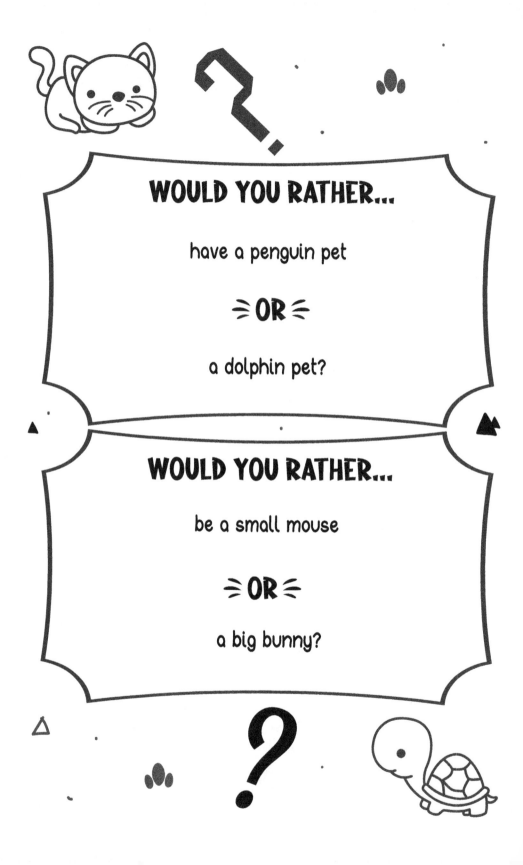

# WOULD YOU RATHER...

have a penguin pet

## ⇒OR⇐

a dolphin pet?

# WOULD YOU RATHER...

be a small mouse

## ⇒OR⇐

a big bunny?

# WOULD YOU RATHER...

visit the zoo

## ⇒ OR ⇐

an amusement park on Easter Monday?

# WOULD YOU RATHER...

choose that animals go extinct

## ⇒ OR ⇐

that plants go extinct?

# School & Learning
# Would You Rather Questions

## WOULD YOU RATHER...

live with nosy and annoying schoolmates

≂ OR ≂

live with nosy and annoying siblings?

## WOULD YOU RATHER...

be the only doctor in the world

≂ OR ≂

be the only teacher in the world?

## WOULD YOU RATHER...

learn how to make popsicles

### ⇒OR⇐

how to make fingerpaint?

## WOULD YOU RATHER...

have 10 times more homework for one month

### ⇒OR⇐

have to do all your weekly homework in one day for three months?

## WOULD YOU RATHER...

rather know too much and have no friends

### ⋚ OR ⋚

know nothing and have many friends?

## WOULD YOU RATHER...

spend your Easter watching the workers in a Hospital

### ⋚ OR ⋚

watching the workers in a Museum?

## WOULD YOU RATHER...

be a businesswoman/businessman

### ⇒OR⇐

a teacher?

## WOULD YOU RATHER...

learn a new thing every minute of your Easter holiday

### ⇒OR⇐

never be able to learn anything?

## WOULD YOU RATHER...

be able to type incredibly fast

## ⋛OR⋚

be able to read very quickly?

## WOULD YOU RATHER...

have to make and share jellybeans with all your classmates

## ⋛OR⋚

help them do all their homework?

## WOULD YOU RATHER...

have lots of toys and not have friends

### ⋚ OR ⋚

have lots of friends and not have toys?

## WOULD YOU RATHER...

spend Easter with your best friend

### ⋚ OR ⋚

spend it with your favorite teacher?

# WOULD YOU RATHER...

be the smartest kid in your school

## ⇒ OR ⇐

the funniest kid in your school?

# WOULD YOU RATHER...

compete in an essay competition

## ⇒ OR ⇐

compete in a science project competition?

# WOULD YOU RATHER...

win a singing talent show

## ⇌OR⇋

a Spelling Bee competition?

# WOULD YOU RATHER...

always have to shout "Happy Easter" to everyone in your school

## ⇌OR⇋

always have to whisper "Happy Easter" to everyone in your school?

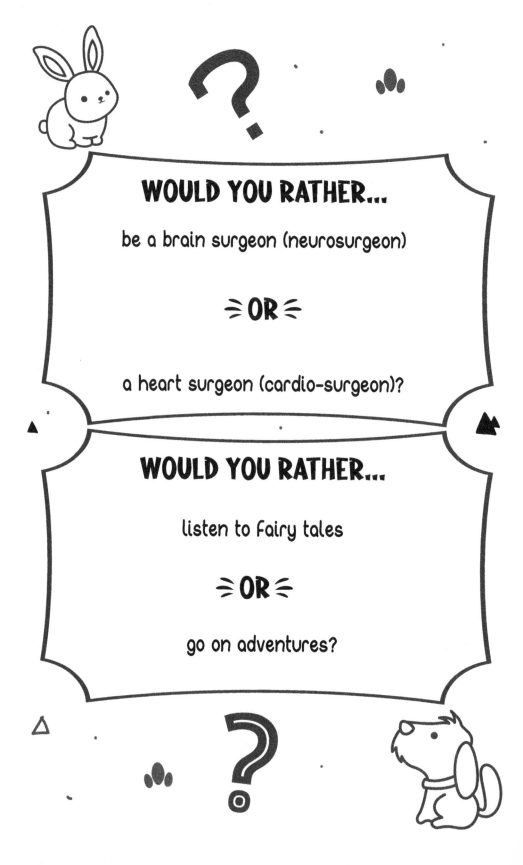

# WOULD YOU RATHER...

be a brain surgeon (neurosurgeon)

≈OR≈

a heart surgeon (cardio-surgeon)?

# WOULD YOU RATHER...

listen to fairy tales

≈OR≈

go on adventures?

## WOULD YOU RATHER...

be stuck in an old and dirty elevator

### ⋛ OR ⋚

be stuck in your school restroom?

## WOULD YOU RATHER...

be really good at science

### ⋛ OR ⋚

really good at sports?

## WOULD YOU RATHER...

be paid 20$ per hour for doing your homework

### ⋛OR⋚
never have any homework?

## WOULD YOU RATHER...

represent your country at the Olympics

### ⋛OR⋚

at an International Science Fair?

## WOULD YOU RATHER...

have an intelligent class teacher and dull colleagues

### ⇒ OR ⇐

have a dull class teacher and intelligent colleagues?

## WOULD YOU RATHER...

miss your school picnic

### ⇒ OR ⇐

summer camp?

## WOULD YOU RATHER...

learn to climb trees

≈ OR ≈

learn to climb rocks?

## WOULD YOU RATHER...

never be able to ask questions

≈ OR ≈

never be able to think before answering them?

## WOULD YOU RATHER...

spend your Easter's eve in detention

### ⇒ OR ⇐

at home without food and internet?

## WOULD YOU RATHER...

be sick for your last week at your old school

### ⇒ OR ⇐

for your first week at your new school?

# Fantasy
# Would You Rather Questions

# WOULD YOU RATHER...

be able to make things appear and disappear

## ≈OR≈

be able to appear and disappear yourself?

# WOULD YOU RATHER...

have a superpower you've always dreamed of

## ≈OR≈

make your favorite cartoon real?

# WOULD YOU RATHER...

live in the previous millennium

## ⋛OR⋚

time travel to the next millennium?

# WOULD YOU RATHER...

be a toddler every Easter

## ⋛OR⋚

be a teenager every Easter?

# WOULD YOU RATHER...

ride on a hot air balloon

## ≈OR≈

ride in a hang glider?

# WOULD YOU RATHER...

visit the moon with a tour space shuttle for Easter

## ≈OR≈

see the Pacific Ocean in a tour submarine for Easter?

## WOULD YOU RATHER...

have your bad dreams and nightmares become real

### ⇒OR⇐

have none of your good dreams and wishes come true?

## WOULD YOU RATHER...

walk through closed doors

### ⇒OR⇐

see through walls?

# WOULD YOU RATHER...

have your own customized robot

## ⋍OR⋍

your own customized video game?

# WOULD YOU RATHER...

have a cave in the mountains

## ⋍OR⋍

a treehouse in the woods?

# WOULD YOU RATHER...

live with aliens in space for 10 years

## ⇒OR⇐

live with spirits in the underworld for 10 years?

# WOULD YOU RATHER...

have the power to imagine things and make them real

## ⇒OR⇐

the power to control people's minds?

# WOULD YOU RATHER...

have a magical broom that could fly

## ⇒OR⇐

a magical carpet that could fly?

# WOULD YOU RATHER...

have the power of an old wizard

## ⇒OR⇐

the flair of a young magician?

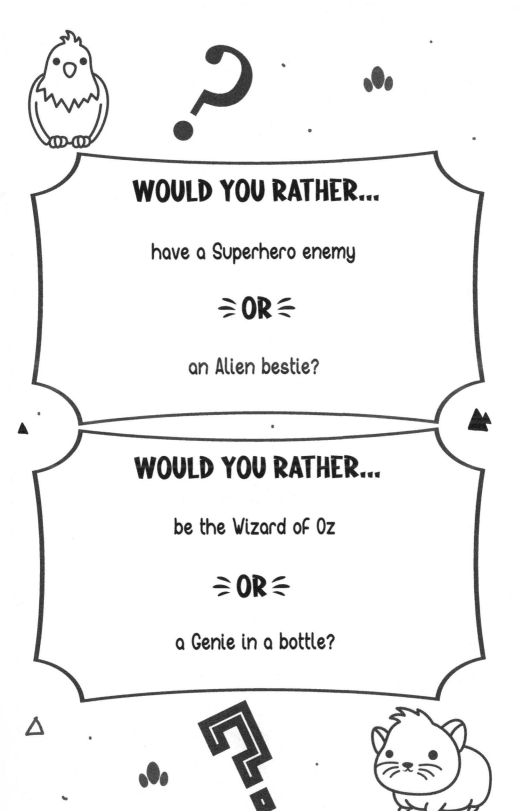

## WOULD YOU RATHER...

have a Superhero enemy

= OR =

an Alien bestie?

## WOULD YOU RATHER...

be the Wizard of Oz

= OR =

a Genie in a bottle?

## WOULD YOU RATHER...

dye the color of your hair

### ⋹OR⋵

change the length of your hair?

## WOULD YOU RATHER...

understand animals speak and not be able
to talk to them

### ⋹OR⋵

talk to animals effectively and not be able
to understand them?

# WOULD YOU RATHER...

make 10 wishes daily for 10 days

## ⇒OR⇐

10 wishes a day, once in every 10 years?

# WOULD YOU RATHER...

have a fast-forward button for your life

## ⇒OR⇐

have a rewind button for your life?

# WOULD YOU RATHER...

move things around with your mind

## ⇒OR⇐

be able to control people with your mind?

# WOULD YOU RATHER...

visit Iceland

## ⇒OR⇐

go sightseeing on the Safari?

# WOULD YOU RATHER...

wear a charm bracelet

## ⋹OR⋹

wear a charm necklace?

# WOULD YOU RATHER...

spend your Easter going to a magical castle
to get 3 wishes that would come true

## ⋹OR⋹

going to a magical forest to get a hidden
treasure chest?

# WOULD YOU RATHER...

have nightmares for a week

## ⇒OR⇐

watch horror movies for a week?

# WOULD YOU RATHER...

have a special room you could fill with as many bubbles as you want, anytime you want,

## ⇒OR⇐

have a slide that goes from your roof to the ground?

Thank you for your purchase and we hope you enjoyed our book!

Your feedback is greatly appreciated as it lets us know how we are doing!

For all inquiries, email us at
ambercitruspress@gmail.com

Amber Citrus Press

Made in the USA
Monee, IL
16 March 2021